Bible Study Series
for junior high/middle school

THE TRUTH ABOUT
GOD

Loveland, Colorado

The Truth About God

Core Belief Bible Study Series

Copyright © 1997 Group Publishing, Inc.

Credits

Editors: Lisa Baba Lauffer and Karl Leuthauser
Managing Editor: Michael D. Warden
Chief Creative Officer: Joani Schultz
Copy Editor: Debbie Gowensmith
Art Director: Lisa Chandler
Cover Art Director: Helen H. Lannis
Cover Designer/Assistant Art Director: Bill Fisher
Computer Graphic Artist: Joyce Douglas
Photographer: Craig DeMartino
Production Manager: Gingar Kunkel

Unless otherwise noted, Scriptures quoted from The Youth Bible, New Century Version, copyright © 1991 by Word Publishing, Dallas, Texas 75039. Used by permission.

ISBN 0-7644-0850-X

10 9 8 7 6 5 4 3 2   06 05 04 03 02 01 00 99 98 97

Printed in the United States of America.

Bible Study Series
for junior high/middle school

contents:

the Core Belief: ▼the Nature of God

The studies in this book attempt to help kids define the ultimately undefinable God. Who is he? What does he do? What's he like? We're not trying to put God in a box, but we want to help kids see God as he has revealed himself through his Word and in their lives. Through these Core Christian Belief studies, young people should begin to understand that God is unique, holy, supremely authoritative over all things, spiritual, relational, active in the world, and redemptive. We want kids to discover that God has distinctive qualities and that he reveals himself in many ways.

the ▼Helpful Stuff

▼the Nature of God as a Core Christian Belief

For young people, modern culture has become a thief, stealing all sense of objective boundaries or moral absolutes. A recent Barna Research Group survey showed that a full 70 percent of young people believe there is no such thing as absolute truth (George Barna, *Generation Next*). Nevertheless, God remains present in kids' lives, reaching out to this generation in need of a safe foundation like a solid rock jutting from an ocean of shifting, uncertain philosophies.

Still, many teenagers feel overwhelmed at the prospect of trying to understand the nature of God. After all, who can begin to comprehend a being so infinitely wise and powerful?

But the truth is that everything your kids do every day is governed by their personal perspective of what God is really like. To comprehend this truth, consider how your young people would live each day if they believed that...

- **God loves only people with blond hair.**
- **God kills people who don't pray three hours each day.**
- **God loves only those who are the best at everything.**
- **God loves people but is really busy running the universe.**

Teenagers who come to believe that God loves them unconditionally no longer feel driven to perform for his approval. Likewise, kids who have accepted God's sovereignty no longer feel the need to be in control of all that happens in their lives. What your kids think about the nature of God shapes almost everything about them.

This study course will help your kids develop a clear image of God's true nature. First, they'll explore God's steadfast love. As they come to understand that God is with them and wants to know them intimately, they'll find comfort for the **loneliness** and isolation they're bound to face as members of a generation of young people who are often left alone and who may feel alienated from those around them.

In the second study, kids will examine God's place amid **life struggles.** Because God sees everything, nothing catches him by surprise. Because God is firmly in control, nothing can frustrate his plans. And because God always knows what's best, we can trust him to lead us even in difficult times.

Kids will then examine the unchanging nature of God the Father in light of the age-old teenager complaint—strained and changing relationships with their **parents.** They'll realize that they can go to their heavenly Father with all their problems, including disagreements and frustrations with parents and stepparents. Kids will find that through these struggles, God is a constant, caring presence.

The final study of this course directs kids to examine the concept of God's righteousness. By coming to terms with the fact that God defines what's right, kids will see the foolishness and sin of participating in dangerous activities such as abusing **inhalants.**

For the teenagers of this generation to survive, they need to stand on the solid foundation that this Core Christian Belief can provide. In a world in which sometimes nothing seems real, understanding God's unchanging nature can provide the one Reality these kids need most.

For a more comprehensive look at this Core Christian Belief, read Group's **Get Real: Making Core Christian Beliefs Relevant to Teenagers.**

DEPTHFINDER HOW THE BIBLE DESCRIBES THE NATURE OF GOD

To help you effectively guide your kids toward this Core Christian Belief, use these overviews as a launching point for a more in-depth study of the nature of God.

● **God is unique in nature.** No person, object, or idea can be compared to God. Therefore, anything we say about God must be based on God's revelation to us. Anything we say about God is expressed in human terms—the only terms we have. The reality of God is always much greater than our minds can understand or express (Psalm 18:25-31; Isaiah 40:12-31; Acts 17:22-29; and Romans 11:33-36).

● **God is the only God.** God is not simply the greatest of gods—God is the only true God (Deuteronomy 4:32-40; Isaiah 45:14-24; 1 Corinthians 8:1-8; and Ephesians 4:1-6).

● **God is holy.** God's holiness sets him apart from all else. Holiness can be described in terms of purity and goodness—but its meaning goes deeper than these words can describe. God is holy and so stands above us in majesty, power, authority, righteousness, and love. Holiness belongs to God alone (Psalm 99:1-9; Ezekiel 20:39-42; 1 Peter 1:15-16; and Revelation 4:1-8).

● **God is the supreme authority over all things**—and he is intimately acquainted with everything he has created. God towers over us as supreme Lord, and yet he is very close as he stoops down to make himself known to us in Jesus Christ (Job 38:1–41:34; Psalm 139; 1 Corinthians 15:12-28; and 1 Timothy 6:13-16).

● **God is eternal.** God has no beginning and no ending (Genesis 21:32-34; Deuteronomy 33:26-27; Romans 16:25-27; and Hebrews 1:10-12).

● **God is spirit.** God is not bound to the material or physical as we are. While he is the one and only God, we know him as three distinct persons: Father, Son, and Holy Spirit. Although each of these "expressions" of God has an individual identity, the three cannot be separated from one another in the common life they share. The work of any one of them always involves the person and work of the other two (Matthew 3:16-17; John 4:24; Galatians 4:4-6; and Titus 3:3-6).

● **God's presence is revealed through his glory.** Glory is the personal manifestation of God's power, righteousness, and love. Sometimes the glory of God is a physical manifestation; sometimes it is a spiritual manifestation (Ezekiel 1:27-28; 10:4; Acts 7:2; and Revelation 21:23).

● **God is intimate.** God isn't an impersonal force, exerting influence in some mechanical, automatic way. He is living and has personal characteristics, just as we do. He forms relationships and has purpose and will (Exodus 3:12-17; Deuteronomy 7:6-8; Daniel 6:26-27; John 6:57; 1 Corinthians 10:13; and 1 Timothy 4:10).

- **God is relational.** God relates to his people as Creator, Ruler, Judge, Deliverer, and Father (Genesis 1:3–2:25; 3:8-24; Deuteronomy 1:29-31; Acts 14:11-17; 1 Corinthians 4:4-5; and Galatians 3:25-27).

- **God has distinctive qualities and attributes.** For example, in the Bible God is described as holy, loving, merciful, gracious, righteous, good, faithful, just, all-knowing, all-powerful, omnipresent (present everywhere at once), personal, jealous, and wrathful against sin (Exodus 34:5-7; 2 Chronicles 19:7; Job 4:17; Ephesians 1:4-8; 1 Thessalonians 5:23-24; and 1 John 1:5-9).

- **God is active in the world.** God is the Creator of all things, and he continues actively working in the world he has created and in the lives of people (1 Samuel 2:6-10; Proverbs 16:33; Acts 4:23-31; and 1 Corinthians 11:12).

- **God is a redeemer.** God makes salvation possible. God is a God of love, a saving God. God has developed and is carrying out a plan of redemption that focuses on his Son, Jesus Christ, as the embodiment of his redemption (2 Samuel 22:1-3; Psalm 49:14-15; Isaiah 25:7-9; Romans 3:20-24; and Philippians 2:5-11).

CORE CHRISTIAN BELIEF OVERVIEW

Here are the twenty-four Core Christian Belief categories that form the backbone of Core Belief Bible Study Series:

The Nature of God	Jesus Christ	The Holy Spirit
Humanity	Evil	Suffering
Creation	The Spiritual Realm	The Bible
Salvation	Spiritual Growth	Personal Character
God's Justice	Sin & Forgiveness	The Last Days
Love	The Church	Worship
Authority	Prayer	Family
Service	Relationships	Sharing Faith

Look for Group's Core Belief Bible Study Series books in these other Core Christian Beliefs!

about

Bible Study Series
for junior high/middle school

Think for a moment about your young people. When your students walk out of your youth program after they graduate from junior high or high school, what do you want them to know? What foundation do you want them to have so they can make wise choices?

You probably want them to know the essentials of the Christian faith. You want them to base everything they do on the foundational truths of Christianity. Are you meeting this goal?

If you have any doubt that your kids will walk into adulthood knowing and living by the tenets of the Christian faith, then you've picked up the right book. All the books in Group's Core Belief Bible Study Series encourage young people to discover the essentials of Christianity and to put those essentials into practice. Let us explain…

What Is Group's Core Belief Bible Study Series?

Group's Core Belief Bible Study Series is a biblically in-depth study series for junior high and senior high teenagers. This Bible study series utilizes four defining commitments to create each study. These "plumb lines" provide structure and continuity for every activity, study, project, and discussion. They are:

● **A Commitment to Biblical Depth**—Core Belief Bible Study Series is founded on the belief that kids not only *can* understand the deeper truths of the Bible but also *want* to understand them. Therefore, the activities and studies in this series strive to explain the "why" behind every truth we explore. That way, kids learn principles, not just rules.

● **A Commitment to Relevance**—Most kids aren't interested in abstract theories or doctrines about the universe. They want to know how to live successfully right now, today, in the heat of problems they can't ignore. Because of this, each study connects a real-life need with biblical principles that speak directly to that need. This study series finally bridges the gap between Bible truths and the real-world issues kids face.

● **A Commitment to Variety**—Today's young people have been raised in a sound bite world. They demand variety. For that reason, no two meetings in this study series are shaped exactly the same.

● **A Commitment to Active and Interactive Learning**—Active learning is learning by doing. Interactive learning simply takes active learning a step further by having kids teach each other what they've learned. It's a process that helps kids internalize and remember their discoveries.

For a more detailed description of these concepts, see the section titled "Why Active and Interactive Learning Works With Teenagers" beginning on page 57.

So how can you accomplish all this in a set of four easy-to-lead Bible studies? By weaving together various "power" elements to produce a fun experience that leaves kids challenged and encouraged.

Turn the page to take a look at some of the power elements used in this series.

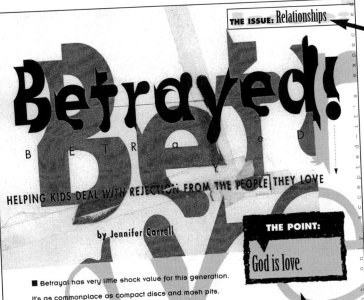

THE ISSUE: Relationships

Betrayed!

HELPING KIDS DEAL WITH REJECTION FROM THE PEOPLE THEY LOVE

by Jennifer Carrell

THE POINT:

God is love.

■ Betrayal has very little shock value for this generation. It's as commonplace as compact discs and mosh pits. For many kids today, betrayal characterizes their parents' wedding vows. It's part of their curriculum at school—it's expected. ■ At the heart of such acceptance lies the belief that nothing is absolute. No vow, no law, no promise can be trusted. Relationships are betrayed at the earliest convenience. Repeatedly, kids see that something called "love" lasts just as long as it's _____ permanence. But deep inside, they hunger to see a

The Study
AT A GLANCE

SECTION	MINUTES	WHAT STUDENTS WILL DO	SUPPLIES
Discussion Starter	up to 5	JUMP-START—Identify some of the most common themes in today's movies.	Newsprint, marker
Investigation of Betrayal	12 to 15	REALITY CHECK—Form groups to compare anonymous, real-life stories of betrayal with experiences in their own lives.	"Profiles of Betrayal" handouts (p. 20), highlighter pens, newsprint, marker, tape
	3 to 5	WHO BETRAYED WHOM?—Guess the identities of the people profiled in the handouts.	Paper, tape, pen
Investigation of True Love	15 to 18	SOURCE WORK—Study and discuss God's definition of perfect love.	Bibles, newsprint, marker
	5 to 7	LOVE MESSAGES—Create unique ways to send a "message of love" to the victims of betrayal they've been studying.	Newsprint, markers, tape
Personal Application	10 to 15	SYMBOLIC LOVE—Give a partner a personal symbol of perfect love.	Paper lunch sack, pens, scissors, paper, catalogs

notes:

● **A Relevant Topic**—More than ever before, kids live in the now. What matters to them and what attracts their hearts is what's happening in their world at this moment. For this reason, every Core Belief Bible Study focuses on a particular hot topic that kids care about.

● **A Core Christian Belief**—Group's Core Belief Bible Study Series organizes the wealth of Christian truth and experience into twenty-four Core Christian Belief categories. These twenty-four headings act as umbrellas for a collection of detailed beliefs that define Christianity and set it apart from the world and every other religion. Each book in this series features one Core Christian Belief with lessons suited for junior high or senior high students.

"But," you ask, "won't my kids be bored talking about all these spiritual beliefs?" No way! As a youth leader, you know the value of using hot topics to connect with young people. Ultimately teenagers talk about issues because they're searching for meaning in their lives. They want to find the one equation that will make sense of all the confusing events happening around them. Each Core Belief Bible Study answers that need by connecting a hot topic with a powerful Christian principle. Kids walk away from the study with something more solid than just the shifting ebb and flow of their own opinions. They walk away with a deeper understanding of their Christian faith.

● **The Point**—This simple statement is designed to be the intersection between the Core Christian Belief and the hot topic. Everything in the study ultimately focuses on The Point so that kids study it and allow it time to sink into their hearts.

● **The Study at a Glance**—A quick look at this chart will tell you what kids will do, how long it will take them to do it, and what supplies you'll need to get it done.

THE POINT OF *BETRAYED!*:

God is love.

THE BIBLE CONNECTION

1 JOHN 4:7-21   The Apostle John explains the nature and definition of perfect love.

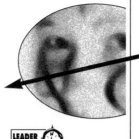

● The Bible Connection—This is the power base of each study. Whether it's just one verse or several chapters, The Bible Connection provides the vital link between kids' minds and their hearts. The content of each Core Belief Bible Study reflects the belief that the true power of God—the power to expose, heal, and change kids' lives—is contained in his Word.

I n this study, kids will compare the imperfect love defined in real-life stories of betrayal to God's definition of perfect love.

By making this comparison, kids can discover that God is love and therefore incapable of betraying them. Then they'll be able to recognize the incredible opportunity God off relationship worthy of their absolute trust.

Explore the verses in The Bible Connection mation in the Depthfinder boxes throughout understanding of how these Scriptures conne

LEADER TIP

THE STUDY

DISCUSSION STARTER ▼

Jump-Start (up to 5 minutes) As kids arrive, ask them to thin common themes in movies, books, TV show have kids each contribute ideas for a mast two other kids in the room and sharing sider providing copies of People maga what's currently showing on television or at th their suggestions, write their respon s on new **come up with a lot of great ide**. **Even tho ent, look through this list and ry to discov ments most of these themes ave in comm**

After kids make several su gestions, mention responses are connected w h the idea of betray

● **Why do you think b trayal is such a co**

Betrayed! 17

LEADER TIP for The Study

Because this topic can be so powerful and relevant to kids' lives, your group members may be tempted to get caught up in issues and lose sight of the deeper biblical principle found in The Point. Help your kids grasp The Point by guiding kids to focus on the biblical investigation and discussing how God's truth connects with reality in their lives.

DEPTHFINDER   UNDERSTANDING INTEGRITY

Your students may not be entirely familiar with the meaning of integrity, especially as it might apply to God's character in the Trinity. Use these definitions (taken from Webster's II New Riverside Dictionary) and other information to help you guide kids toward a better understanding of how God maintains integrity through the three expressions of the Trinity.

Integrity: 1. Firm adherence to a code or standard of values. 2. The state of being unimpaired. 3. The quality or condition of being undivided.

Synonyms for integrity include probity, completeness, wholeness, soundness, and perfection.

Our word "integrity" comes from the Latin word *integritas*, which means soundness. *Integritas* is also the root of the word "integer," which means "whole or complete," as in a "whole" number.

The Hebrew word that's often translated "integrity" (for example, in Psalm 25:21 [NIV]) is *tam*. It means whole, perfect, sincere, and honest.

CREATIVE GOD-EXPLORATION ▼

Top Hats (18 to 20 minutes) Form three groups, with each trio member from the previous activity going to a different group. Give each group Bibles, paper, and pens, and assign each group a different hat God wears: Father, Son, or Holy Spirit. their goal is to write one list describing what God does in the

● Depthfinder Boxes—These informative sidelights located throughout each study add insight into a particular passage, word, historical fact, or Christian doctrine. Depthfinder boxes also provide insight into teen culture, adolescent development, current events, and philosophy.

● Leader Tips—These handy information boxes coach you through the study, offering helpful suggestions on everything from altering activities for different-sized groups to streamlining discussions to using effective discipline techniques.

holy Profiles

Your assigned Bible passage describes how a particular person or group responded when confronted with God's holiness. Use the information in your passage to help your group discuss the questions below. Then use your flashlights to teach the other two groups what you discover.

■ Based on your passage, what does holiness look like?

■ What does holiness sound like?

■ When people see God's holiness, how does it affect them?

■ How is this response to God's holiness like humility?

■ Based on your passage, how would you describe humility?

■ Why is humility an appropriate human response to God's holiness?

■ Based on what you see in your passage, do you think you are a humble person? Why or why not?

■ What's one way you could develop humility in your life this week?

● Handouts—Most Core Belief Bible Studies include photocopiable handouts to use with your group. Handouts might take the form of a fun game, a lively discussion starter, or a challenging study page for kids to take home— anything to make your study more meaningful and effective.

The Last Word on Core Belief Bible Studies

Soon after you begin to use Group's Core Belief Bible Study Series, you'll see signs of real growth in your group members. Your kids will gain a deeper understanding of the Bible and of their own Christian faith. They'll see more clearly how a relationship with Jesus affects their daily lives. And they'll grow closer to God.

But that's not all. You'll also see kids grow closer to one another.

That's because this series is founded on the principle that Christian faith grows best in the context of relationship. Each study uses a variety of interactive pairs and small groups and always includes discussion questions that promote deeper relationships. The friendships kids will build through this study series will enable them to grow *together* toward a deeper relationship with God.

never ALONE

GoD'S ULTiMaTe ANSWeR To LoNELiNeSS

by Lisa Baba Lauffer

■ Do you know what it's like to feel lonely? Remember the isolation, the sorrow, the fear of never being loved? ■ Multiply that by a hundred, and you've got your young people. ■ Studies suggest that teenagers struggle with loneliness at a rate 50 to 100 percent higher than adults. Wondering if anyone

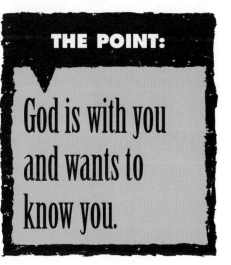

THE POINT:

God is with you and wants to know you.

will ever know or care about them, they walk around with an assumed identity, aching inside, desperate for someone to see beyond the mask and love them for who they really are.■ Somebody does. ■ This study explores the wonder of God's intimate knowledge of us in order to help kids discover God's loving presence in the face of loneliness.

The Study
AT A GLANCE

SECTION	MINUTES	WHAT STUDENTS WILL DO	SUPPLIES
Creative Opener	15 to 20	INSIDE OUT—Create poster board boxes that represent who they are.	Bible, poster board, scissors, markers, tape
Bible Discovery	15 to 20	GOD KNOWS EVERY BODY—Create visual representations of God's intimate knowledge of us and constant presence among us as expressed in Psalm 139.	Bibles, newsprint, markers, tape
Devotion	15 to 20	SEARCH AND KNOW—Listen to Psalm 139 while standing back to back or while maintaining eye contact with a partner.	Bibles, markers, tape

notes:

God is with you and wants to know you.

THE BIBLE CONNECTION

PSALM 139   David writes about his intimate relationship with God.

I n this study, kids will create representations of themselves and of God's presence with and knowledge of them as described in Psalm 139. Through this experience, kids can discover that even when they feel lonely, they still have a Friend who knows them intimately, loves them completely, and will never leave them.

Explore the verses in The Bible Connection, then examine the information in the Depthfinder boxes throughout the study to gain a deeper understanding of how these Scriptures connect with your young people.

BEFORE THE STUDY

Create a cross pattern from poster board. Cut a five-by-five-inch square from one corner of the poster board, and use it as a guide to draw a cross on the remaining poster board. Draw an outline of a cross four squares long and three squares wide. Then cut along the lines to create the cross. Refer to the "Box Creation" illustration below to see how to do this. You'll use the cross pattern during the study to create a box.

LEADER TIP for The Study

Whenever you tell groups to discuss a list of questions, write the questions on newsprint and tape the newsprint to a wall so groups can answer the questions at their own pace.

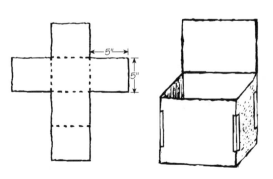

5"
5"

THE STUDY

CREATIVE OPENER ▼

Inside Out

(15 to 20 minutes)

After kids arrive, say: **Today we're going to discuss loneliness. To start, find a space to yourself, and sit down on the floor. Close your eyes, and think of how you feel when you're lonely.** Allow kids thirty seconds to think. Then say: **Keep your eyes closed, and continue to think about being lonely while I read parts of Psalm 139 to you.** Read aloud Psalm 139:1-18, 23-24.

Say: **To explore loneliness, we're going to create boxes that represent who we are.** Using the pattern you made before the study, have students draw and cut cross shapes from poster board.

After students create their crosses, have them fold their crosses into boxes. Refer to the "Box Creation" illustration (p. 17) to show kids how to do this. After kids have practiced folding their boxes, have them unfold their boxes so the poster board looks like a cross made from six squares.

Have each student find an open space on the floor. Give each student a marker, and say: **I'm going to ask you some questions. Write or draw your answer to each question on a different square "inside" your cross. Leave the two bottom squares blank for now. As you answer these questions, remember that no one else will read what you've written.** Ask:

- **What are five words you would use to describe yourself?**
- **Where do you like to go to be alone?**
- **When are you most likely to feel lonely?**
- **What do you do when you're lonely?**

After answering these questions, students should have two blank squares left on their crosses. Have kids fold their crosses into boxes again. Have them tape the sides but leave the "lids"—which should be blank squares—open to write on later in the study.

Have kids form two circles, one inside the other. Have each student

DEPTH FINDER UNDERSTANDING THE BIBLE

When Jesus Christ endured the cross, he also endured the ultimate loneliness: complete separation from God (see Matthew 27:45-46). To take our sins upon himself, he had to sacrifice his intimate communion with God the Father. Because of Jesus Christ's selfless sacrifice, we *never* have to experience that depth of loneliness. Though others may betray or abandon us, God is *always* with us.

stand face to face with a partner from the other circle. If you have an uneven number of students, join in the activity to make the circles even.

Say: **Now I'm going to ask you another set of questions. Write your answer to each question on a different "outside" square of your box. After you write your answer, share it with your partner from the other circle.** Ask:

● **Where do you go to be with friends?** After kids write and share their answers with their partners, have the inside circle rotate one person to the right. Ask:

● **What do you like to do when you're with friends?** After kids write and share, have the outside circle rotate two spaces to the left. Ask:

● **How do you feel when you're with friends?** After kids write and share, have both circles rotate one space to the left. Ask:

● **What do you look for in a friend?** After kids write and share, have the outside circle rotate one space to the left. Ask:

● **What's the best thing about having friends?** After kids write and share, have the inside circle rotate two spaces to the right.

Say: **Hand your box to the person across from you. On the last blank square on the outside of your partner's box, write one positive thing that makes your partner fun to be with. For example, you could write, "You're really smart" or "You have a great sense of humor."**

Have kids return the boxes to their owners. Then have kids form trios to discuss these questions:

● **How is hiding the answers inside your box like being lonely? How is it different?**

● **How is sharing the answers outside your box like being lonely? How is it different?**

● **How is hiding or sharing your answers like inviting God to know you?**

● **How is unfolding your box like opening yourself up to Jesus?**

Say: **Sometimes we feel lonely, even when we have plenty of friends. Through the rest of this study, we're going to learn that even in lonely times <u>God is with you and wants to know you.</u>**

LEADER TIP for The Study

Consider creating a Loneliness Hot Line with your students. Have students volunteer to serve as Loneliness Hot Line counselors, people willing to talk and pray with students who need a friend. Type a list of volunteers' names and phone numbers, and give a copy to everyone in your group.

You may even consider extending the Loneliness Hot Line to a local middle school or junior high school. Consult a trusted professional counselor to train your students as peer counselors, and make sure you cover all the legal bases.

BIBLE DISCOVERY ▼

God Knows Every Body (15 to 20 minutes)

Say: **Often we feel lonely because we think no one knows who we truly are. Sometimes we feel lonely because we think no one wants to be around us. But the truth is <u>God is with you and wants to know you.</u>**

Give each trio newsprint and markers. Say: **Have the person in your trio with the shortest first name lie down on the newsprint. Then draw an outline of that person's body on the newsprint.** After trios have completed this, say: **In your trios, read Psalm 139. As you read this passage, watch for clues that tell you what God knows about you and where God is.** After trios have read the passage, say: **Inside your "body," write all the things that God knows about you according to Psalm**

LEADER TIP

for The Study

If you have a student who is struggling through loneliness, talking it out usually will help him or her overcome it. However, at times it is appropriate to refer a student for professional counseling. Consider referring a student to counseling if he or she

● seems to feel hopeless,

● seems to feel more lonely over time, or

● uses his or her relationship with you as his or her primary source of friendship.

DEPTHFINDER — UNDERSTANDING THESE KIDS

Kids don't have to be alone to feel lonely. Sometimes they feel loneliest in the middle of a crowd. Desperate to fit in and win friends, young people may compromise their unique personalities—their interests, the way they dress, even their strongest beliefs. Eventually, kids who compromise realize their "friends" really don't know them and possibly don't want to.

That can be one of life's loneliest moments.

Psalm 139 speaks to the basic human desire to be known deeply. Despite their best efforts, your young people cannot hide their true selves from God. God, though busy running the universe, knows your kids' favorite bands, how they're doing in school, and when they feel lonely. In God, the One who knows them intimately and never leaves them, your kids can find the ultimate caring Friend.

139. Outside your "body," write all the places God is according to Psalm 139. Read the passage again if you need to. After trios have finished, have them tape their "bodies" to one wall. Allow time for everyone to read what the other trios discovered.

Have trios re-form and discuss these questions:

● **When you feel lonely, what do you need the most?**

● **What's your reaction to what Psalm 139 says about God knowing you? about being with you?**

● **How can Psalm 139 help you when you're feeling lonely?**

On one of the blank squares inside their boxes, have kids write one thing they learned from Psalm 139 that could help them the next time they feel lonely.

Say: **As Psalm 139 says, <u>God is with you and wants to know you.</u> God created you, he knows everything about you, and he's all around you. God is an ever-present Friend.**

Where can I go to get a w a y from your Spirit?
Where can I r^un from you?

psalm **139** 7-10

If I go up to the heavens, you are there.
If I lie _{down} in the grave, you are there.
If I ^{rise} with the sun in the east
and settle in the west beyond the sea,
even there you would guide me.
With your right hand you would HOLD me.

Search and Know

(15 to 20 minutes)

Say: **We've just studied Psalm 139 to learn how God knows us and is with us. Now we're going to experience this passage in another way.**

Form two groups, and direct the groups to opposite sides of the room. Name one group the Ears and the other group the Eyes. Have kids in both groups form pairs. Instruct the partners in Ear pairs to stand back to back and alternate reading the verses of Psalm 139 to each other. Have the partners in Eye pairs look at each other while you read Psalm 139 aloud to them. The Eyes must maintain eye contact without talking, laughing, or looking away.

After the experience, have each Ear pair join with an Eye pair to form a foursome and discuss these questions:

● **What's your reaction to this experience?**

● **Ears, how is hearing Psalm 139 while standing back to back with your partner like God knowing and being with you?**

● **Eyes, how is hearing Psalm 139 while watching your partner like God knowing and being with you?**

● **Now that you know that <u>God is with you and wants to know you,</u> how do you want to interact with God every day? on days when you're lonely?**

Say: **<u>God is with you and wants to know you.</u> How will you respond to that today? You should have one empty square left inside your box. On that empty square, write your response to today's study. You could rewrite a part of Psalm 139 to remind you that God is with you. You could write a question that you'll think and pray about during the coming week. Or you could write one way you'll commit to responding when you feel lonely.**

DEPTH FINDER   UNDERSTANDING THESE KIDS

Therapist and author Les Parrott III defines loneliness as "the painful awareness that we are not meaningfully connected with others." Adolescents seem particularly prone to loneliness; studies have found that 15 to 20 percent of all adolescents deal with painful loneliness (as compared to only 10 percent of the adult population).

Why are adolescents more likely to feel lonely? Here are some factors:

● the mobility of our society, which separates teenagers from friends and family members;

● changes (sometimes negative) in their relationships with their parents;

● emotional development that leads to a greater need for intimacy;

● a desire to have their developing, unique identities accepted;

● unrealistic comparisons to friends and celebrities, which magnify feelings of failure and rejection; and

● a need to feel important and significant with no place to meet this need.

After kids write their responses, have them finish taping their boxes shut. Encourage kids to take their boxes home and place them in a prominent spot to remind them of what they learned.

DEPTHFINDER

UNDERSTANDING THE BIBLE

If one of your students expresses that he or she feels lonely, copy this Depthfinder and encourage that student to read it and study the listed Bible passages. Your kids can combat their loneliness by learning how God helped Bible heroes conquer their loneliness.

BIBLE HERO	WHY THIS BIBLE HERO WAS LONELY	HOW GOD HELPED THIS BIBLE HERO CONQUER LONELINESS	HOW GOD CAN HELP YOU, TOO
Hannah (1 Samuel 1:3-20)	Hannah was unable to bear a child and was often taunted by another woman who had children.	God answered Hannah's prayers for a child by giving her Samuel.	God can answer your prayers for help and companionship.
Elijah (1 Kings 19:1-18)	Queen Jezebel wanted to kill Elijah, and Elijah had to run for his life.	God sent an angel to give Elijah food and drink. God also spoke directly to Elijah.	God can fulfill your needs—even your need to hear from him directly.
Paul (2 Timothy 4:16-18)	Imprisoned, Paul awaited execution alone after his "friends" had abandoned him.	God stayed with Paul and gave him strength to share his faith.	God is with you and will give you strength to make it through your loneliness.
JESUS CHRIST (Matthew 26:36-46)	Jesus felt the anguish of knowing he would be crucified.	God allowed Christ to endure his lonely time and his death so that he might rise again, saving all of us from sin and separation from God.	God will never abandon you because Jesus already endured that loneliness for you.

MAKING SENSE

making sense ● making sense ● making sense

MAKING SENSE

in a
World
Gone Mad

by Bob Buller

THE POINT:

God is in control and knows what he's doing.

■ Today's kids live in a chaotic and uncertain world. Broken and blended families, violence on the streets and in the schools, poverty, unwanted pregnancies, abusive parents, pressure to conform, and media images assault them from every side. ■ Fortunately, the chaos is more apparent than real. God stands in the midst of this world's insanity, calmly and consistently accomplishing his will. Because God sees everything, nothing catches him by surprise. Because God is firmly in control, nothing can frustrate his plans. And because God always knows what's best, we can trust him to lead us even in chaotic times. ■ This study encourages kids to trust God during chaotic times by helping them see how God can transform the worst of situations into something good.

The Study
AT A GLANCE

SECTION	MINUTES	WHAT STUDENTS WILL DO	SUPPLIES
Experiential Opening	2 to 5	PUZZLE MANIA—Try to put together a puzzle while wearing blindfolds.	"Person-Shaped Puzzle" handout (p. 33), blindfolds
	2 to 5	LIFE'S A PUZZLE—Compare putting a puzzle together to understanding their lives.	
Bible Discovery	10 to 15	STEPHEN'S STORY—Tell the story of Stephen's life in coded messages.	Bibles, newsprint, markers, tape, paper, pencils
	5 to 10	THE REST OF THE STORY—Discover how God completed the puzzle of Stephen's life through his death.	Bibles, marker, newsprint
Bible Application	5 to 10	MY CHAOS, GOD'S WISDOM—Learn how God can turn their chaotic situations into good things.	Markers, index cards
	5 to 10	I'M PRAYING FOR YOU—Ask God to help others deal with the chaos in their lives.	Markers
Creative Closing	5 to 10	PIECES OF MY PUZZLE—Affirm each other for dealing with chaos in positive ways.	"Person-Shaped Puzzle" handouts (p. 33), pencils

notes:

THE POINT OF *MAKING SENSE IN A WORLD GONE MAD:*

God is in control and knows what he's doing.

THE BIBLE CONNECTION

ACTS 6:8-15; 7:51—8:8   God uses Stephen's death to spread the gospel.

JAMES 1:2-5   James encourages us to ask God for wisdom so we can learn from life's trials.

PROVERBS 3:5-6   God directs the lives of people who trust in him.

In this study, kids will work together to try to assemble a puzzle while blindfolded. Then they'll compare this to the way God helps us put the puzzles of our lives together even when we can't see what he's doing.

Through this comparison, kids can learn to trust God even when life seems chaotic.

Explore the verses in The Bible Connection, then study the information in the Depthfinder boxes throughout the study to gain a deeper understanding of how these Scriptures connect with your young people.

LEADER TIP
for The Study

Whenever you ask groups to discuss a list of questions, write the list on newsprint and tape it to a wall so groups can discuss the questions at their own pace.

BEFORE THE STUDY

Photocopy and cut apart the "Person-Shaped Puzzle" from page 33.

List various chaotic situations that junior high kids might face. Write each situation on a separate sheet of paper, and hang the papers around the room. For example, you might write situations such as the following:

● Your parents divorce.
● You have problems at school.
● You break up with your boyfriend or girlfriend.
● You go to a new school.
● Your parent loses a job.
● A friend dies.
● You move to a new community.
● You get into trouble with the police.
● You lose a friend.
● You run away from home.

Make one photocopy of the "Person-Shaped Puzzle" handout (p. 33) for each group member.

THE STUDY

EXPERIENTIAL OPENING ▼

LEADER TIP

for Puzzle Mania

Although the puzzle has seven pieces, the activity will work for a group of any size. If you have puzzle pieces left after you give each person one piece, distribute the extra pieces so some kids have more than one. If you have more than seven kids in your group, make several copies of the handout, and have kids attempt to put several puzzles together at the same time.

Puzzle Mania
(2 to 5 minutes)
Blindfold everyone, and give each person a piece of the Person-Shaped Puzzle. Tell kids they have three minutes to put the puzzle together on the floor. Kids can talk to one another and try to put the pieces together by feeling the edges, but they cannot remove their blindfolds. If kids assemble the puzzle within the three minutes, omit the second discussion question and modify the instructions in "Life's a Puzzle."

After three minutes, call time and instruct kids to remove their blindfolds.

Life's a Puzzle
(2 to 5 minutes)
Form groups of four, and instruct group members to discuss these questions:

● **What was it like trying to put a puzzle together without seeing?**

● **How long do you think it would take you to put the puzzle together in this way?**

● **How is putting this puzzle together like putting together the "pieces" of your life?**

● **In what ways is your life like a puzzle? In what ways is it different?**

● **What things make it hard for you to put together the pieces of your life?**

Say: **Sometimes our lives are so full of chaos and uncertainty that we feel out of control. We don't know how all the pieces of our lives fit together or even if we have all the pieces. We'll learn today, however, that no matter how confusing life seems to us, <u>God is in control and knows what he's doing.</u>**

BIBLE DISCOVERY ▼

LEADER TIP

for Life's a Puzzle

If you had kids try to put together an incomplete puzzle, ask:

● **How is a puzzle with missing pieces like your life? unlike your life?**

Stephen's Story
(10 to 15 minutes)
Say: **Sometimes it's hard to see that God is in control of our lives when we're in the middle of chaotic situations. However, we can often see what God has been doing after all the pieces come together. To learn how to put the puzzle pieces of our lives together, let's examine the puzzle of Stephen's life.**

Have the kids in each foursome number off from one to four. Have them form new groups: Send all the Ones to one area of the room, the Twos to another area, and so on. Instruct each group to read one of these four passages: Acts 6:8-10; Acts 6:11-15; Acts 7:51-56; and Acts 7:57–8:1.

While the groups are reading, draw a five-piece puzzle on a sheet of newsprint (see diagram in the margin). Write "Acts 6:8-10" on one piece, "Acts 6:11-15" on another, and so on. (You'll write in the blank area later in the activity.) Then write the following questions in the appropriate areas of the puzzle, and hang the newsprint where everyone can see it.

● Who was Stephen? (Acts 6:8-10)
● What was Stephen's situation? (Acts 6:11-15)
● What was Stephen's response? (Acts 7:51-56)
● What happened to Stephen? (Acts 7:57–8:1)

Say: **Just as there are different kinds of chaotic experiences, there are different kinds of puzzles. A code is one kind of puzzle. Let's use coded messages to solve the puzzle of Stephen's life.**

Instruct each group to compose a one-sentence answer to its assigned question and then "translate" the answer into a coded message. Assign the following codes to the groups.

● Ones: A=2, B=4, C=6, and so on
● Twos: A=26, B=25, C=24, and so on
● Threes: A=0, B=1, C=2, and so on
● Fours: A=25, B=24, C=23, and so on

After groups have translated their answers into code, have them write the coded messages on the appropriate sections of the newsprint. Then give each group a sheet of paper and a pencil, and have groups race to decipher other groups' messages.

After five minutes, have groups reveal messages that haven't been deciphered. Then have kids return to their original groups of four and discuss these questions:

● **What was difficult about trying to break the code?**
● **How is this like what Stephen might have felt in his situation?**
● **What parts of Stephen's life seem to have been chaotic?**
● **How did Stephen respond to the chaos in his life?**

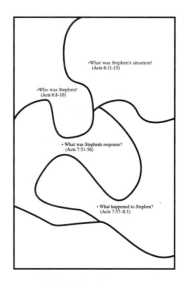

LEADER TIP

for Stephen's Story

If you want groups to translate their answers into the coded messages more quickly, consider writing out each code on a sheet of paper and giving each group the appropriate code.

Making Sense in a World Gone Mad 29

LEADER TIP

for Stephen's Story

If kids have trouble deciphering the codes, offer to help them. For example, you could tell kids that M equals twenty-six in the Ones' message, fourteen in the Twos' message, twelve in the Threes' message, and thirteen in the Fours' message. After another minute, you could add that S equals thirty-eight in the Ones' message, eight in the Twos' message, eighteen in the Threes' message, and seven in the Fours' message.

LEADER TIP

for My Chaos, God's Wisdom

Encourage kids to put their symbols on as many situation papers as apply to them, but assure them that they don't need to mark any that they would prefer to keep private. Also, you may want to provide blank sheets of paper, a marker, and tape so kids can add any situations you might have forgotten. Tell kids to write any chaotic situation you've missed on a sheet of paper and hang it near the other papers.

● How would you have reacted if you had been in Stephen's situation?

● Do you think Stephen knew how the pieces of his life fit together? Explain.

● How are you like Stephen? How are you unlike him?

● To what extent was Stephen's life out of his control? out of God's control?

● Why do you think God let Stephen be killed?

● Why do you think God lets chaotic things happen in your life?

(5 to 10 minutes)

The Rest of the Story

Say: **Contrary to what we might expect, the puzzle of Stephen's life wasn't finished when he died. There was still one important piece to be put into place. In your group, read Acts 8:1-8 to discover what that piece was.**

While groups are reading, write, "Acts 8:1-8" on the blank puzzle piece on the newsprint. Ask:

● **What good came out of Stephen's death?**

Write kids' responses in the appropriate space on the newsprint. Then say: **Stephen probably didn't understand why God let him die, but Stephen did know that <u>God is in control and knows what he's doing.</u> God used the chaos of Stephen's life and death to draw others to Christ. He can use the chaotic situations of your life to accomplish something good, too.**

BIBLE APPLICATION ▼

My Chaos, God's Wisdom

(5 to 10 minutes)

Distribute markers of various colors and index cards. Tell kids to draw on the cards symbols that somehow represent who they are. For example, one person might draw a happy face because he likes to smile, while another might sketch a tennis shoe because she plays racquet sports.

After kids create their symbols, instruct them to walk around, read the chaotic situations that you hung around the room before the study, and draw their symbols on the papers that describe situations in their lives. Give kids at least three minutes to put their symbols on the situation papers.

Then have kids re-form their original foursomes and discuss these questions in their groups:

● **How does it feel to be surrounded by so many chaotic situations?**

● **What did this activity reveal about your life? the lives of others in the group?**

● **How is the chaotic appearance of the papers like the chaotic appearance of our lives? How is it different?**

● **Based on all this chaos, how can we know that <u>God is in control and knows what he's doing?</u>**

DEPTHFINDER   STEPHEN'S LIFELINE

Since Stephen's name is Greek (*Stephanos*: crown, reward), it's almost certain that he was a Hellenistic Jew. As such, he probably grew up in a non-Jewish, Greek-speaking environment. Like Jews raised in Palestine, he would have maintained Jewish religious convictions, but he would have accepted Greco-Roman cultural practices more easily than they. As a result, he would have been more universal in his understanding of God's love for humans than many Jews of his day.

The book of Acts describes Stephen as "a man with great faith and full of the Holy Spirit" and "richly blessed by God who gave him the power to do great miracles and signs" (Acts 6:5, 8). The early church recognized Stephen's gifts and abilities and appointed him to a group of seven who administered the daily distribution of food to the widows (Acts 6:1-6).

Stephen is best remembered, however, as the early church's first martyr. A problem arose when certain Hellenistic Jews from the synagogue of Free Men falsely accused Stephen of teaching against the temple and the law of Moses. Stephen defended himself before the Sanhedrin (the Jewish high court) by demonstrating from history that God had never needed a temple and that the Jews had always rejected God's leaders. When Stephen accused his listeners of killing God's preeminent leader (Jesus), the Sanhedrin took Stephen outside the city and stoned him to death.

LEADER TIP for The Study

Because this topic can be so powerful and relevant to kids' lives, your group members may be tempted to get caught up in issues and lose sight of the deeper biblical principle found in The Point. Help your kids grasp The Point by guiding them to focus on the biblical investigation and by discussing how God's truth connects with reality in their lives.

Instruct groups to read Proverbs 3:5-6 and James 1:2-5. Then have group members discuss the following questions:

● **Can you think of a time you went through a chaotic situation that God turned into something good? Explain.**

● **How can God turn our chaotic experiences into good things?**

● **What can God's wisdom do for us when we're going through chaotic times?**

Say: **Everyone has to deal with chaos in his or her life. But Christians can ask God for the wisdom to survive and even thrive in chaos. And whether or not we ever understand why we go through difficult times, we can always be certain that <u>God is in control and knows what he's doing.</u>**

I'm Praying for You
(5 to 10 minutes) Give everyone a marker. Say: **On the back of your index card, write one chaotic situation you're currently facing.**

Give kids a moment to do this. Then say: **Now write a question you'd like God to answer about that situation. For example, you might want God to help you understand why you're going through the situation or what you're supposed to do. If you don't mind someone else knowing about your situation, sign your card. If you prefer, you may use your symbol or leave your card unsigned. When you're finished writing, put your card with the others in a pile in the center of the room.**

After everyone has put a card in the pile, mix the cards. Have everyone take a card (not his or her own), find a private area, and pray for the situation and the question written on the card. Encourage kids to take their cards home as reminders to pray for one another and for the chaotic situations they all face.

LEADER TIP
for Pieces of My Puzzle

To ensure that everyone gets affirmed, encourage kids to write on as many papers as they can, and write your own positive comments on papers that don't have many.

CREATIVE CLOSING ▼

Pieces of My Puzzle (5 to 10 minutes)

Give each person a pencil and a copy of the "Person-Shaped Puzzle" handout (p. 33). Have kids write their names at the top of their puzzles and place them on a table. Instruct each student to write affirmations on at least five different puzzles. Have kids describe on each puzzle one positive way that person deals with chaos. When kids finish writing, say: **The pieces of your life's puzzle will probably change as you grow and change. Take your puzzle home to remind yourself that life is never as chaotic as it seems because God is in control and knows what he's doing.**

DEPTHFINDER UNDERSTANDING THE BIBLE

When James promises that God will give "wisdom" to anyone who asks for it, he probably is referring to wisdom in the midst of troubles (see James 1:2-4). At the very least, God will show us how to respond when we face troubles. God may also help us understand the nature and the purpose of our struggles. However, we may never *fully* comprehend why God allows us to undergo trials. For example, Job never understood why his world crumbled. Whatever our level of understanding, we should trust God and his goodness at all times.

PERSON-SHAPED PUZZLE

a Parent change

helping kids rely on God as their families change

by Lisa Baba Lauffer

THE POINT:

God never changes.

■ "My mom is *so* not cool!" "Can you believe my stepdad thought he could ground me?" "My dad wants me to spend the weekend with him, but he's never around when I really need him." ■ Junior highers face a tough transition, and their parents are along for the ride. As your students stretch the boundaries of their independence, their relationships with their parents change. Their parents, who used to be their sole source of comfort, are now the bane of their existence, embarrassing them at every turn or forbidding them from doing something they really want to do. ■ And those are just the developmental aspects of junior higher/parent relations. Add to that today's context for family relationships—divorce, abandonment, remarriage—and they become even more complex. Kids from broken homes experience separation from one parent or the other at all times. Often, they must adjust to a stepparent who makes new rules for them to abide by. And sadly, many of these kids have parents who avoid them or refuse to pay child support. ■ Your students are growing and changing. Their relationships with their parents are also developing and transforming. How will your young people navigate these treacherous waters? By relying on their heavenly Father who never changes. This study will show them how.

The Study
AT A GLANCE

SECTION	MINUTES	WHAT STUDENTS WILL DO	SUPPLIES
Family Evaluation	25 to 30	LIVING FAMILY PHOTO ALBUM—Create "family photos" using other students to represent changes in their relationships with their parents.	"God Never Changes" handouts (p. 45), tape or stapler, various skit props
Bible Exploration	20 to 25	CHILDREN OF THE HEAVENLY FATHER—Explore Bible passages that describe God as unchanging and as a heavenly Father, then create a future living family photo based on what they learn in Scripture.	Bibles, "God Never Changes" handouts (p. 45), pencils
Response	5 to 10	ATTENTION, PARENTS AND STEPPARENTS!—Write open letters to the parents and stepparents in the church.	Paper, pencils, tape

notes:

God never changes.

THE BIBLE CONNECTION

NUMBERS 23:19; MALACHI 3:6A; JAMES 1:17-18	These passages express that God never changes.
PSALM 103:13; PROVERBS 3:11-12; ISAIAH 43:1-7; MATTHEW 7:9-11	These passages describe God as a parent.

I n this study, kids will create "snapshots" of times that their relationships with their parents changed. Then they'll explore Bible passages that describe God as a heavenly Father who never changes.

Through this experience, kids can realize that they can rely on God for everything they need from a parent while giving their parents some slack to learn and grow.

Explore the verses in The Bible Connection, then examine the information in the Depthfinder boxes throughout the study to gain a deeper understanding of how these Scriptures connect with your young people.

BEFORE THE STUDY

Make one photocopy of the "God Never Changes" handout (p. 45) for every four students in your class. Then fold each handout in half with the printing on the inside. Tape or staple the handouts so they remain folded.

LEADER TIP
for The Study

Whenever you ask groups to discuss a list of questions, write the list on newsprint and tape it to a wall so groups can discuss the questions at their own pace.

THE STUDY

LEADER TIP
for Living Family Photo Album

If possible, have an adult leader join each group to guide discussion and to help with living picture poses and caption ideas. If you're short on adult leaders, have your adult leaders circulate among the groups to help as needed.

FAMILY EVALUATION ▼

Living Family Photo Album

(25 to 30 minutes)

After everyone has arrived, say: **Today we're going to talk about our parents and stepparents. Our relationships with our parents and stepparents are tough. We often fight with them, but sometimes we get along great. Some of you may have painful feelings about your parents and stepparents. Others of you may feel great about them. So as we discuss parents**

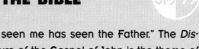

DEPTHFINDER — UNDERSTANDING THE BIBLE

In John 14:9, Jesus says, "Whoever has seen me has seen the Father." The *Disciple's Study Bible* states that one feature of the Gospel of John is the theme of Jesus as the revealer of the Father. Jesus reveals that the Father...

● wants his children to follow him (1:43).
● knows his children (1:47-48).
● brings enjoyment to his children (2:7-10).
● gets angry when his children disobey him (2:13-19).
● cares about his children's eternal well-being (3:1-8, 16-21).
● cares for all his children's spiritual needs (4:7-24).
● heals his children's hurts—physical and spiritual (5:1-14).
● always takes care of his children (5:16-17).
● provides for his children's physical needs (6:1-13).
● never drives away those he loves (6:37).
● cares more about his children than about empty rituals (7:21-24).
● provides his children with the Holy Spirit to give them life (7:37-39).
● forgives his children for their sins (8:1-11).
● leads and protects his people (10:11-15).
● hurts when his children hurt (11:35).
● enjoys the gifts his children give him (12:3-8).
● serves his children (13:2-5).
● knows the hearts of his children (13:36-38).
● prepares a place in heaven for his children and prepares a way for them to get there (14:1-7).
● does not leave his children alone but provides for them a helper, the Holy Spirit (14:16-18, 25-27).
● loves his children so much that he sacrificed his Son (19:16-18, 30).

If your students want to know more about God the Father, encourage them to study the Scriptures above.

DEPTH FINDER — UNDERSTANDING THE BIBLE

We call God our heavenly Father, but what does that really mean? According to the *Disciple's Study Bible*, God is a Father in three different senses. First, he's the Father of Jesus Christ because he sent Jesus to earth as a human. Second, God is the Father of all Christians because he redeems us and adopts us as his sons and daughters when we accept his gracious gift of eternal life. And finally, God is the Father of everyone because he's our creator. God acts as a Father "in his personal concern for all people, his protective watchcare over his people, and in redemption, nurture, and discipline in the lives of Christians."

LEADER TIP for The Study

Because this topic can be so powerful and relevant to kids' lives, your group members may be tempted to get caught up in issues and lose sight of the deeper biblical principle found in The Point. Help your kids grasp The Point by guiding them to focus on the biblical investigation and by discussing how God's truth connects with reality in their lives.

and stepparents today, remember that others don't have your same experiences. Offer each other patience and understanding.

Have kids form foursomes. Then say: **To begin our study, we're going to create "living family photo albums." Think of one family-changing situation you've experienced in your life: a circumstance that changed your relationship with your parents or stepparents. This situation can be a happy or sad time. For example, your relationship with your mom might have changed when she remarried. This relationship-changing situation doesn't necessarily have to revolve around you. For example, maybe your relationship with your dad changed when a younger brother had to stay in the hospital.**

Give kids a minute to think of their situations. As they think, set out a variety of skit props such as clothes, hats, and sports equipment. Also hand each group one of the folded handouts. Then say: **In your groups, choose one person to be the Family Historian. Each person in the group will eventually have a turn as the Family Historian. When it's your turn, you'll express the situation that changed your relationship with one or both of your parents or with a stepparent. But you'll do this in a unique way. You'll use your group members to create a "living picture" of your situation. For example, if you want to express that a relationship-changing event was when your mom remarried, you could have two group members pose as the bride and groom, one person pose as a sister who's the flower girl, and place yourself in the picture wherever you feel you belong.**

You may use any of the props I've supplied, and you *must* use the paper I handed your group as a prop. For example, you might roll it up and use it as a bouquet of flowers at a wedding or fold it and use it as a get-well card in a hospital. You can use it any way you'd like, but don't open it up until I tell you to do so.

Once you've set up your living picture, tell your group members what the caption beneath this picture would say and why. In our first example, you might say, "The day I adopted a dad" because you feel you gained a father.

Allow groups twenty minutes to create their living photo albums, with each student sharing one living picture. In five minute intervals, tell groups to switch Family Historians to keep the activity moving and to allow everyone a turn.

After everyone has had a turn to share his or her living picture, have foursomes discuss these questions:

● **How is your relationship with your parents or stepparents?**

● **Has your relationship with your parents or stepparents ever changed? If so, were the changes a result of a parent or stepparent changing? the result of you changing? Explain.**

Say: **Open the handout you used in your living family photo albums. Continue to answer the questions in your group.**

● **Does the message at the top of the handout affect your reactions to the changes in your relationships with your parents or stepparents? Why or why not?**

● **How was the constant presence of the handout—and the message at the top of it—in your living pictures like God's unchanging presence in your family? How was it different?**

When groups have finished, invite kids to express to the class their responses to the last question. Then say: **As we grow, our families change—especially in regards to our relationships with our parents and stepparents. But <u>God never changes</u>, and he's our heavenly Father.**

Every good action and every perfect gift is from **God**. These good gifts come down from the **Creator** of the sun, moon, and stars, who does not change like their shifting shadows. **God** decided to give us life through the **word of truth** so we might be the most important of all the things **he** made.

James 1:17-18

Let's explore this a bit more to discover how our unchanging heavenly Father helps us endure our changing relationships with our parents and stepparents. But before we do, let's pray that God will lead our discovery time. Pray: **Dear God, you know that we often struggle in our relationships with our parents and stepparents. You know that we often have difficulties adjusting to some of the changes we experience in those relationships. Please use your Word to teach us what we need to know to endure these changes. Amen.**

LEADER TIP

for Children of the Heavenly Father

To help the discussion move smoothly, make sure each student has a Bible, and encourage groups to assign one or two Scriptures for each student to look up and read aloud.

BIBLE EXPLORATION ▼

Children of the Heavenly Father (20 to 25 minutes)

Hand each group a pencil, and have groups go through their "God Never Changes" handouts (p. 45). (Have extra handouts available in case groups ruined their handouts during the previous activity.)

After ten minutes, invite groups to share some of their responses to the handout questions. Say: **God never changes, and that means he'll always be our heavenly Father with all the loving characteristics you've discovered in the Bible passages. And God**

DEPTHFINDER UNDERSTANDING FATHERS

Fathers get blamed for a lot these days. And some of the blame is justified—many fathers fail to be available for their kids. Some fathers leave their kids before the kids are born, choosing not to marry the mothers. Others are absent due to divorce or frequent business travel. Still others are present in body but unavailable emotionally or spiritually for their kids.[1] Researchers have found that dads spend an average of seven and one-half minutes with their teenagers every *week*.[2] And of every five teenagers from divorced homes, only two have fathers who send child-support payments for them.[3]

However, many dads today are doing the job right. Today's "family man" considers cooking, changing diapers (of course, not for teenage children!), and staying home with sick kids a part of his duties. Fathers are finding a new intimacy with their kids as they involve themselves in the daily requirements of parenting. Fathers approach these tasks in their own unique ways, creating a loving family environment everyone enjoys. Both moms and dads appreciate team parenting, and very few would return to the days when parents divided the tasks along gender lines.[4]

[1] Jim Burton, "Father Absence: a National Epidemic," Home Life magazine (October 1995), as summarized in Current Thoughts & Trends magazine (December 1995), 12.

[2] "Dad Who?", Group Magazine (June-August 1990).

[3] "Divorce Robs Kids' Pockets," Group Magazine (June-August 1991).

[4] Catherine Cartwright, "The New Family Man," Working Mother magazine (June 1995), 28-30, as summarized in Current Thoughts & Trends magazine (August 1995), 10.

cares about the changes you experience in your family. Some of you are going through some tough times with your parents and stepparents. Maybe you argue with your mom and dad a lot when you used to get along with them really well. Or maybe you don't like a stepparent because you have really different personalities.

In your groups, create another living family picture. This time, create a picture of how your family could be in the future with your heavenly Father making some changes. Base the changes God could make in your family upon what you learn from the Bible passages. Don't forget to use the handout as a prop! Once you've created your picture of the future, say what the caption beneath the picture would say and why.

Allow groups five minutes to create their new photos and share their captions.

RESPONSE ▼

Attention, Parents and Stepparents! (5 to 10 minutes)

Say: **When our relationships with our parents and stepparents change, we can feel discouraged. Maybe we liked the way things were. Maybe we struggle with adjusting to new rules and roles. But God never changes, and one of his unchanging characteristics is his ability to help us. He can help us adjust to new circumstances.**

Hand each group a sheet of paper and a pencil. Say: **Just as changing relationships with parents and stepparents are difficult for us to endure, they're difficult for your parents and stepparents, too. So in your group, write an encouraging letter to all parents and stepparents out there. We'll display these letters in the foyer of the church. Tell the parents and stepparents what they're doing right and how the God who never changes can carry them through the changes they experience. Also tell them what you'll do to make positive changes in your own families. You may choose whether or not to put your name on your letter.**

LEADER TIP

for Attention, Parents and Stepparents!

To help kids with this activity, write the instructions on a sheet of newsprint, and post it where everyone can see it.

Give groups about five minutes to create their letters. Then either collect the letters to put in the church foyer later, or lead everyone to the church foyer and have kids tape their letters to a wall. When you've finished collecting the letters or the students have finished taping the letters to a wall, pray: **Heavenly Father, thank you for taking care of us as your children. Thanks for being a constant presence we can rely on. Please be with our parents and stepparents, and help them through the changes we're experiencing as we all grow and change. Help us to encourage them. And remind us that through whatever struggles we experience in our relationships with our parents and stepparents, you're always there to guide us through those struggles. Thank you, amen.**

Before dismissing the class, have each student turn to a partner and tell that person one thing that will help that person endure changes or make positive changes in his or her family. For example, someone might say, "Your kind spirit will help your family peacefully adjust to the changes you experience."

In your group, read the following passages: Numbers 23:19; Malachi 3:6a; and James 1:17-18. Then discuss these questions:

● What do these passages say about God?

● How does the fact that **God never changes** affect how you feel about your parents and stepparents? about some of the changes you've experienced in your relationships with your parents and stepparents?

Read James 1:17-18 again. What does this passage say that our unchanging God gives us? Does this affect your view of your changing relationships with your parents or stepparents? Why or why not?

Now read Psalm 103:13; Proverbs 3:11-12; Isaiah 43:1-7; and Matthew 7:9-11. List below the characteristics you discover about God as your heavenly Father.

_____

_____

_____

_____

_____

_____

_____

_____

_____

Having read those passages and made your list, discuss these questions:

● How is God like your parents and stepparents? different from them?

● What can God give you as a Father that your earthly parents and stepparents can't?

● How does the fact that **God never changes** affect his role as our heavenly Father? affect your ability to rely on him?

● Do you wish some things would change in your relationships with your parents? with your stepparents? If so, what? How could God as your loving, heavenly Father help change those things?

a Deadly aroma

Discovering God's View on Inhalants

by Karl Leuthauser

THE POINT:

God defines what is right.

■ They are cheap and accessible. Their use is even more prevalent than the use of marijuana and hashish by junior highers. They produce a quick and intense high, and one out of every five eighth-graders has abused them.[1] ■ Inhalants have become the "drug of choice for junior highers."[2] ■ Inhalants may be invisible, but the long-term damage they cause is not. Inhalant use can cause paranoia, brain damage, and even death.[3] Even first-time users are susceptible to these risks. This study can show you how to prevent these tragedies from happening to your kids.

The Study
AT A GLANCE
AT A GLANCE

SECTION	MINUTES	WHAT STUDENTS WILL DO	SUPPLIES
Dramatic Introduction	15 to 20	SET THE STAGE—Produce a skit that introduces the topic of inhalants and the need to discern right from wrong.	Bibles, "Set the Stage" handouts (p. 54), index cards, newsprint, markers, tape, scissors
Creative Study	5 to 10	FOUNDATIONAL FILTERS—Create filters that help them discern right from wrong.	Bibles, "Foundational Filters" handouts (p. 55), coffee filters, pencils, permanent markers
	10 to 15	JAVA JOURNEY—Use coffee and filters to demonstrate how God's nature is a filter for our decisions.	Cups, masking tape, plastic spoons, markers, can of coffee, can opener, bucket, water, paper, rubber bands, newspaper
Logical Conclusion	15 to 20	TRIAL OF THE SCENTURY—Put inhalants on trial.	"Trial Briefings" handouts (p. 56)

notes:

God defines what is right.

THE BIBLE CONNECTION

EXODUS 20:13-17; MATTHEW 5:21-22	God wants us to avoid hurting others.
DEUTERONOMY 30:11-14; PSALM 25:8-9; 34:8; PROVERBS 14:12; MATTHEW 19:17-19	God shows us how we can determine the difference between right and wrong.
PSALM 121:5-6; PROVERBS 18:10	God keeps us safe.
ISAIAH 48:17-18; JEREMIAH 29:11	God wants the best for us.
ACTS 17:27; EPHESIANS 3:12	God wants us to seek him.

I n this study, kids will investigate some of the filters God has given us to discern right from wrong and then will apply those filters to inhalant use.

Through this investigation, kids can discover that inhalant use goes against God's nature because it harms his creation. They can learn that he desires them to make choices that benefit themselves and others. They can find that, because God defines what is right, he wants them to follow his example.

Explore the verses in The Bible Connection, then examine the information in the Depthfinder boxes throughout the study to gain a deeper understanding of how these Scriptures connect with your young people.

LEADER TIP for The Study

Whenever groups discuss a list of questions, write the list on newsprint and tape it to a wall so groups can discuss the questions at their own pace.

BEFORE THE STUDY

Prepare an index card for each student in the group. On six of the index cards write "Actor." On the remaining index cards, write "Stage Crew."

Fill a bucket with water and set it aside. Open the can of coffee, then wrap a piece of paper around the can. On the piece of paper, write "Situations."

THE STUDY

DRAMATIC INTRODUCTION ▼

Set the Stage (15 to 20 minutes)

As kids arrive, give each one an index card. Make sure you distribute all of the Actor cards.

Say: **To start off our time today, we're going to perform a skit. Look at your cards to see the part you're going to play. In a moment, I'll give each of you a copy of the skit. The Actors should read through it, decide who will fill each role, and determine how to follow the stage directions. The Stage Crew should use markers, newsprint, and the description of the setting found at the top of the handout to create a backdrop for the skit.**

Distribute the "Set the Stage" handout (p. 54), and have kids get into the Actors and Stage Crew groups. If you choose to provide props, give them to the Actors. Give a large sheet of newsprint, markers, tape, and scissors to the Stage Crew. Give the groups about five minutes to prepare. Then ask the Stage Crew to tape the backdrop they created to a wall. Have the Actors perform the skit for the Stage Crew. When the skit is over, call the kids back together. Ask:

- **Did Shelly's dad make a fair decision? Why or why not?**
- **Did Shelly make the right decision? Explain.**
- **Have you ever tried to make the right decision but still got in trouble for what you did or didn't do? Explain.**
- **How can we tell when a decision is right or wrong?**

Say: **Some people may think that Shelly made the wrong decision by having those particular friends over in the first place. Some may think that Shelly's dad isn't being fair at all. Sometimes it's difficult to know what's right. We all see things from our own perspective, and we usually feel that our perspective is the correct one. However, this doesn't mean that we always make the best choices.**

Have students form four groups. Tape a sheet of newsprint to a wall, then list these verses on it: Deuteronomy 30:11-14; Psalm 34:8; Proverbs 14:12; and Matthew 19:17-19. Under the verses write the following questions:

- **What encouragement or instruction does God give in this passage?**
- **According to this passage, how can we know right from wrong?**

Assign one verse to each group, and instruct the groups to discuss the questions on the newsprint. Tell the groups to be prepared to share what they discovered. When groups finish their discussions, have the kids come back together. Then ask a representative from each group to share its discoveries.

Have a volunteer read Psalm 25:8-9 aloud. Then say: **When we face difficult decisions, we can look to God because**

LEADER TIP for Set the Stage

To make the skit more lively, gather props for kids to use. Some suggested items include a mirror, a comb, a sock, a can of hair spray, and a telephone. As soon as you determine who will be Actors, give them the items. Tell the Actors that they need to figure out how to use the props in the skit.

LEADER TIP for Set the Stage

This skit is designed for six participants. If you have exactly six kids, don't distribute the index cards; instead, just have everyone be Actors. If you have fewer than six kids, have the Narrator also perform the Caseworker's part, and, if necessary, perform a part yourself.

he defines what is right. He will show us the right way
even when our own perspective makes the choice difficult. If
Scripture isn't clear on a specific issue we face, we can look at
God's character to give us direction. Let's look at some examples.

CREATIVE STUDY ▼

Foundational Filters

(5 to 10 minutes)
Have the kids get into groups of four; then ask
group members to number off from one to four. Give each student a coffee filter, a pencil, and a "Foundational Filters" handout (p. 55). Then
give one permanent marker to every group. Ask kids to complete the
sections on the handout that correspond with their numbers.

When the kids finish, say: **Share what you've discovered with the
rest of your group. Then write your answer to letter "C" on each
group member's coffee filter. You should have four attributes of
God's character written on your filters when you're finished.**

When groups finish, say: **Look at your filter. Can you think of any
other characteristics of God's nature that might help you make the
right choice in a difficult situation? Share it with your group, and
write it on your filter.**

Java Journey

(10 to 15 minutes)
Say: **When we're in difficult situations and the Bible
doesn't give clear direction, we can look at God's nature to
help us decide because <u>God defines what is right.</u> Let me**
show you what I mean.

Give each student a cup, a marker, a piece of masking tape, and a
plastic spoon. Ask kids to write their names on their pieces of tape and
then put the tape on their cups. Put the can of coffee labeled "Situations"
and the bucket of water in the center of the room.

Then say: **The cup symbolizes you; the coffee represents the situations that force you to make decisions. Get a spoonful of situations. Pour the situations into your cup. The water symbolizes your
life. Put a spoonful of water in your cup for every year you have
been alive. Now let's try the same thing using the filters God has
given us.**

Have kids set the dirty cups aside. Give each student a rubber band
and another cup. Have kids insert their coffee filters at least an inch into
the new cups and fasten them to the top of their cups with the rubber
bands.

Say: **You can use God's character as a filter for making decisions.
You can ask yourself questions when you're in a situation and you
need to decide what to do. For example, if you know that God
wants you to become closer to him, you can ask, "Does this choice
bring me closer to God?" before you decide. If you know that he's
concerned with your safety, you could ask, "Will this hurt me?"
before you take a risk. According to your filter, what are some
other questions you could ask before you make a decision?**

**LEADER
TIP**
for Foundational
Filters

Have the kids put
newspaper under their
coffee filters before
they write on them.
Otherwise the ink will
leave a permanent
stain on the writing
surface.

**LEADER
TIP**
for Java Journey

If you don't want to
use up a lot of coffee,
you can have each
group share one filter
and two cups. Instruct
kids to write their an-
swers to letter "C" on
the group filter and
then explain their
answers to the rest of
the group. Ask groups
to write "you" on the
pieces of tape that
they place on their
cups.

LEADER TIP

for The Study

Because this topic can be so powerful and relevant to kids' lives, your group members may be tempted to get caught up in issues and lose sight of the deeper biblical principle found in The Point. Help your kids grasp The Point by guiding them to focus on the biblical investigation and by discussing how God's truth connects with reality in their lives.

Instruct the kids to share their answers with their groups. Then have students put one spoonful of coffee in their filters and then put in one spoonful of water for every year they have been alive. Ask kids to carefully remove the filters and look in their cups. Ask:

- **What's the difference between the two cups?**
- **How's the filter like God's character?**
- **Was the filter completely effective?**
- **Can understanding God's character keep you from making poor choices? Why or why not?**

Say: **Even when we do our best to make good decisions, we still make mistakes. We can't completely filter sin out of our lives by the choices we make. Making decisions that are in accordance with God's character can help us avoid sin because he defines what is right. Jesus knew that sin would still sneak through our filters, so he died for us so that we may have forgiveness.**

Have kids return to their groups to pray for each other. Encourage kids to ask God for the wisdom to make right choices in difficult situations and for guidance about areas in their lives in which they need to make different choices. Tell them to ask God to help them in those areas.

When kids finish, have them clean their filters and cups in the bucket of water and then set their filters on newspaper.

Say: **Let's look at a practical way we can use the filters God has given us by looking at the situation found in the skit. Shelly's friend wanted to use the hair spray to get high. In this next activity, let's evaluate this situation and use our filters to decide what's right.**

LOGICAL CONCLUSION ▼

LEADER TIP

for Trial of the Scentury

If you only have four kids or if kids are having a high-energy meeting, fill the Judge and Bailiffs roles yourself. That way you'll be able to keep the trial moving and help the kids focus.

Trial of the Scentury

(15 to 20 minutes)

Tell kids that they're going to put inhalants on trial. Have students form five groups. Distribute the "Trial Briefings" handout (p. 56). Assign the following roles to different groups: the Judge and Bailiffs, the Defense team, Dr. Huffenoser's team, the Jury, and the Prosecution team. Give them five minutes to prepare for their roles. As

DEPTHFINDER   WHAT'S ALL THE FUSS?

As the kids in your group investigate the morality of inhalants, you may want to volunteer some additional information. While using inhalants, kids may experience a variety of symptoms including dizziness, disorientation, loss of consciousness, fatigue, headaches, chronic cough, chest pains, shortness of breath, and abdominal pain.

From little or frequent use, kids may encounter long-term side effects including burns, hearing damage, poor breathing, bone marrow damage, hepatitis, chronic cough, and coma.

groups finish preparing, make sure that the Bailiffs have set up the courtroom. Ask the Bailiffs to show the other groups where they are to sit. Then ask the Judge to begin the trial. After the Jury has delivered its verdict, call the group together. Ask:

● **Do you agree with the Jury's decision? Why or why not?**

● **What tools other than our filters has God given us to decide what is right and wrong?**

Say: **When we must decide whether something is right or wrong, we should check the Bible for guidance. When the Bible isn't clear on a situation we face, we can look at God's character to help us make the best decision. He defines what is right, and we can look at his nature to help us make the right choices.**

[1]Unless otherwise noted, all factual information and statistics are from "What Communities Can Do About Inhalant Abuse," International Institute on Inhalant Abuse, 1995.

[2]Rick Lawrence, "Kids Deadly Love Affair With Inhalants," Jr. High Ministry Magazine, August 1993.

[3]"Inhalants: A Dangerous Experiment," Brown University Child and Adolescent Behavior Letter, May 1995.

SET THE STAGE

THE SETTING

The skit takes place on Shelly's front porch. Shelly is sitting on a chair. She's holding a hand mirror, a comb, and a can of hair spray. It's a warm summer day. The sun is shining and birds are chirping. There's a clothesline with shirts, sheets, and socks hanging from it. The door to the house is open, and the screen door is closed.

THE SKIT

(Shelly sits on a chair; the Narrator stands.)

Narrator: Shelly was sitting on her front porch, fixing her hair. It was the first Saturday in a long time that she didn't have to wake up at seven. A few of her friends were coming over to hang out and to celebrate what seemed to be her first free weekend since forever. While she was waiting for her friends to arrive, she thought about how many garbage sacks she had filled with crumpled paper and cigarette butts. She thought about how glad she was that she wasn't wasting her weekend picking up trash with a loser work crew. She thought about what her caseworker told her the day she was sentenced for possession of pot.

(Caseworker enters.)

Caseworker: Shelly, the judge wanted to send you to a rehabilitation center for girls, but I told her that you were sincere when you said that you would stay out of trouble. I stuck my neck out for you when I recommended that you get community service instead. Don't make me sorry that I took that risk for you. If you get into anything that even smells like trouble in the next six months, I'll recommend that they send you to the rehab center without thinking twice about it.

(Caseworker exits.)

Narrator: Shelly wanted to stay out of trouble and hang out with her friends. She made up her mind to keep away from drugs. The sun was shining, and for the first time in a while, Shelly felt content.

(Friends One and Two enter.)

Narrator: Shelly's friends arrived. After some hugs and some small chat, they ran into a problem.

Friend One: So what do you want to do today?

Friend Two: Let's go to the mall.

Shelly: We always go to the mall. How about going to a movie?

Friend Two: What's playing?

Friend One: Nothing.

Friend Two: We could play on the computer.

Friend One: Whatever.

Narrator: Shelly and her friends spent about ten minutes trying to come up with something to do. They couldn't think of anything that sounded fun. They were about to give up when Shelly's friend took a sock from the clothesline and picked up Shelly's hair spray.

Friend One: *(Picks up hair spray and sock.)* Shelly, do you want to go first?

Shelly: I don't think so. I can't get caught messing around with that stuff.

Friend Two: What are you going to do with that?

Friend One: Don't be stupid. You sniff it, just like glue.

Friend Two: Oh, yeah.

(Dad enters.)

Narrator: Just as they finished talking, Shelly's dad came out through the front door. He stopped short and his mouth dropped open.

Dad: Shelly, it's time for your friends to go. Tell them goodbye and come inside.

(Dad exits.)

Friend Two: Bummer. What's he going to do?

Shelly: I don't know.

Friend One: I'm sorry, Shelly. I hope you're not in too much trouble.

(Friends One and Two exit; Dad enters.)

Narrator: Just as Shelly's friends were leaving, her dad came out to the porch with a cordless phone and handed it to Shelly.

Dad: Shelly, I want you to explain what just happened.

Shelly: To who?

Dad: To your caseworker, Shelly.

Shelly: I can't believe you called my caseworker! They'll send me to the rehab center for sure.

Dad: Young lady, I'm doing this for your own good!

Foundational Filters

ONES:

A. Look up Proverbs 18:10 and Psalm 121:5-6.

B. What benefit does God offer to those who trust in him?

C. According to these verses, what does God want *for* us? Use the marker to write your answer on the coffee filter.

TWOS:

A. Look up Isaiah 48:17-18 and Jeremiah 29:11.

B. According to the passage in Isaiah, what's the result of obeying God?

C. According to these verses, what does God want us to have? Use the marker to write your answer on the coffee filter.

THREES:

A. Look up Exodus 20:13-17 and Matthew 5:21-22.

B. What's one common thread between the commands you've read?

C. According to these verses, how does God want us to act toward other people? Use the marker to write your answer on the coffee filter.

FOURS:

A. Look up Acts 17:27 and Ephesians 3:12.

B. Since God is everywhere, why does it sometimes feel like we are far away from him?

C. According to these verses, what does God want us to do? Use the marker to write your answer on the coffee filter.

Trial Briefings------

(cut those dotted lines)

JUDGE AND BAILIFFS

Elect a Judge. Everyone else in the group is a Bailiff. The Bailiffs are responsible for carrying out the Judge's orders and for setting up the courtroom. The courtroom should be set up as follows: Place two chairs side by side against a wall for the Judge and witness stand; place chairs for the Jury to one side of the Judge and witness-stand chairs; and place chairs for the Prosecution team and the Defense team opposite the Jury.

The Judge should keep the trial moving. He should explain that each team will take a turn and that both teams must be silent when the other team is speaking. Don't be afraid to yell out, "Order in the court!" if one team interrupts the other. Begin by asking Dr. Huffenoser to come to the witness stand. Ask the Defense team if they have any questions for Dr. Huffenoser. After they ask the questions, have them give their closing arguments. When they finish, ask the Prosecution team if they have any questions for the doctor. Then give them a chance to give their closing arguments. When both teams are done, ask the Jury to make a decision.

DEFENSE TEAM

You're trying to prove that inhalant use isn't wrong. Explain that it's not illegal to purchase the items necessary for inhalant use. Argue that most kids have a pretty good time when they use inhalants and that God wants us to have fun. Begin your case by asking Dr. Huffenoser to explain why kids would want to use inhalants. Then use one of the coffee filters a group member made to argue that inhalant use doesn't violate God's attitudes toward us. For example, you might argue that using inhalants doesn't prevent people from drawing near to God.

JURY

Before the trial, pick a coffee filter that someone in your group created. Use this filter to guide you as you decide if inhalant use is right or wrong. Listen carefully to what the doctor and the lawyers say, discuss your opinions, then take a vote. Remember that you need to find only one violation of God's nature to find inhalant use wrong. Pick someone to announce your decision to the class. Make sure you explain why you found inhalant use to be right or wrong.

DR. HUFFENOSER'S TEAM

Pick one person to be Dr. Huffenoser. Everyone else in the group will be Research Assistants. The assistants' job is to help Dr. Huffenoser prepare what he or she is going to say during the trial. The doctor is an expert on the subject of inhalants (even though his or her Research Assistants do all the work). The doctor doesn't really care if inhalant use is right or wrong. The doctor just wants to tell the court everything he or she knows so that he or she can become a famous and respected expert.

Dr. Huffenoser should know that kids use inhalants for a variety of reasons. The most common reasons are that inhalants...

- are cheap,
- are easy to get,
- produce intense highs,
- can produce hallucinations,
- can make kids lightheaded, and
- can cause kids to get excited and lose their sense of danger.

Dr. Huffenoser should also know that inhalant use produces various side effects that may include...

- brain damage,
- heart damage,
- poor breathing,
- death,
- liver damage, and
- violent behavior while high.

Dr. Huffenoser can bring this handout to help him or her while on the witness stand.

PROSECUTION TEAM

You are trying to prove that using inhalants is wrong. You feel that using inhalants goes against God's character and what he wants for his people. You feel that inhalants don't help people grow closer to God in any way. You are also concerned with the risk they pose to the safety of the user and to the safety of others. Begin your statement by asking Dr. Huffenoser to explain the serious side effects of inhalants. Then compare inhalants with a coffee filter that someone in your group created.

why ▼Active and Interactive Learning works with teenagers

Let's Start With the Big Picture

Think back to a major life lesson you've learned.
Got it? Now answer these questions:
● Did you learn your lesson from something you read?
● Did you learn it from something you heard?
● Did you learn it from something you experienced?

If you're like 99 percent of your peers, you answered "yes" only to the third question—you learned your life lesson from something you experienced.

This simple test illustrates the most convincing reason for using active and interactive learning with young people: People learn best through experience. Or to put it even more simply, people learn by doing.

Learning by doing is what active learning is all about. No more sitting quietly in chairs and listening to a speaker expound theories about God—that's passive learning. Active learning gets kids out of their chairs and into the experience of life. With active learning, kids get to *do* what they're studying. They *feel* the effects of the principles you teach. They *learn* by experiencing truth firsthand.

Active learning works because it recognizes three basic learning needs and uses them in concert to enable young people to make discoveries on their own and to find practical life applications for the truths they believe.

So what are these three basic learning needs?
1. Teenagers need action.
2. Teenagers need to think.
3. Teenagers need to talk.

Read on to find out exactly how these needs will be met by using the active and interactive learning techniques in Group's Core Belief Bible Study Series in your youth group.

1. Teenagers Need Action

Aircraft pilots know well the difference between passive and active learning. Their passive learning comes through listening to flight instructors and reading flight-instruction books. Their active learning comes through actually flying an airplane or flight simulator. Books and lectures may be helpful, but pilots really learn to fly by manipulating a plane's controls themselves.

We can help young people learn in a similar way. Though we may engage students passively in some reading and listening to teachers, their understanding and application of God's Word will really take off through simulated and real-life experiences.

Forms of active learning include simulation games; role-plays; service projects; experiments; research projects; group pantomimes; mock trials; construction projects; purposeful games; field trips; and, of course, the most powerful form of active learning—real-life experiences.

We can more fully explain active learning by exploring four of its characteristics:

● **Active learning is an adventure.** Passive learning is almost always predictable. Students sit passively while the teacher or speaker follows a planned outline or script.

In active learning, kids may learn lessons the teacher never envisioned. Because the leader trusts students to help create the learning experience, learners may venture into unforeseen discoveries. And often the teacher learns as much as the students.

● **Active learning is fun and captivating.** What are we communicating when we say, "OK, the fun's over—time to talk about God"? What's the hidden message? That joy is separate from God? And that learning is separate from joy?

What a shame.

Active learning is not joyless. One seventh-grader we interviewed clearly remembered her best Sunday school lesson: "Jesus was the light, and we went into a dark room and shut off the lights. We had a candle, and we learned that Jesus is the light and the dark can't shut off the light." That's active learning. Deena enjoyed the lesson. She had fun. And she learned.

Active learning intrigues people. Whether they find a foot-washing experience captivating or maybe a bit uncomfortable, they learn. And they learn on a level deeper than any work sheet or teacher's lecture could ever reach.

● **Active learning involves everyone.** Here the difference between passive and active learning becomes abundantly clear. It's like the difference between watching a football game on television and actually playing in the game.

The "trust walk" provides a good example of involving everyone in active learning. Half of the group members put on blindfolds; the other half serve as guides. The "blind" people trust the guides to lead them through the building or outdoors. The guides prevent the blind people from falling down stairs or tripping over rocks. Everyone needs to participate to learn the inherent lessons of trust, faith, doubt, fear, confidence, and servanthood. Passive spectators of this experience would learn little, but participants learn a great deal.

● **Active learning is focused through debriefing.** Activity simply for activity's sake doesn't usually result in good learning. Debriefing— evaluating an experience by discussing it in pairs or small groups— helps focus the experience and draw out its meaning. Debriefing helps sort and order the information students gather during the experience. It helps learners relate the recently experienced activity to their lives.

The process of debriefing is best started immediately after an experience. We use a three-step process in debriefing: reflection, interpretation, and application.

Reflection—This first step asks the students, "How did you feel?" Active-learning experiences typically evoke an emotional reaction, so it's appropriate to begin debriefing at that level.

Some people ask, "What do feelings have to do with education?" Feelings have everything to do with education. Think back again to that time in your life when you learned a big lesson. In all likelihood, strong feelings accompanied that lesson. Our emotions tend to cement things into our memories.

When you're debriefing, use open-ended questions to probe feelings. Avoid questions that can be answered with a "yes" or "no." Let your learners know that there are no wrong answers to these "feeling" questions. Everyone's feelings are valid.

Interpretation—The next step in the debriefing process asks, "What does this mean to you? How is this experience like or unlike some other aspect of your life?" Now you're asking people to identify a message or principle from the experience.

You want your learners to discover the message for themselves. So instead of telling students your answers, take the time to ask questions that encourage self-discovery. Use Scripture and discussion in pairs or small groups to explore how the actions and effects of the activity might translate to their lives.

Alert! Some of your people may interpret wonderful messages that you never intended. That's not failure! That's the Holy Spirit at work. God allows us to catch different glimpses of his kingdom even when we all look through the same glass.

Application—The final debriefing step asks, "What will you do about it?" This step moves learning into action. Your young people have shared a common experience. They've discovered a principle. Now they must create something new with what they've just experienced and interpreted. They must integrate the message into their lives.

The application stage of debriefing calls for a decision. Ask your students how they'll change, how they'll grow, what they'll do as a result of your time together.

2. Teenagers Need to Think

Today's students have been trained not to think. They aren't dumber than previous generations. We've simply conditioned them not to use their heads.

You see, we've trained our kids to respond with the simplistic answers they think the teacher wants to hear. Fill-in-the-blank student workbooks and teachers who ask dead-end questions such as "What's the capital of Delaware?" have produced kids and adults who have learned not to think.

And it doesn't just happen in junior high or high school. Our children are schooled very early not to think. Teachers attempt to help kids read with nonsensical fill-in-the-blank drills, word scrambles, and missing-letter puzzles.

Helping teenagers think requires a paradigm shift in how we teach. We need to plan for and set aside time for higher-order thinking and be willing to reduce our time spent on lower-order parroting. Group's Core Belief Bible Study Series is designed to help you do just that.

Thinking classrooms look quite different from traditional classrooms. In most church environments, the teacher does most of the talking and hopes that knowledge will transmit from his or her brain to the students'. In thinking settings, the teacher coaches students to ponder, wonder, imagine, and problem-solve.

3. Teenagers Need to Talk

Everyone knows that the person who learns the most in any class is the teacher. Explaining a concept to someone else is usually more helpful to the explainer than to the listener. So why not let the students do more teaching? That's one of the chief benefits of letting kids do the talking. This process is called interactive learning.

What is interactive learning? Interactive learning occurs when students discuss and work cooperatively in pairs or small groups.

Interactive learning encourages learners to work together. It honors the fact that students can learn from one another, not just from the teacher. Students work together in pairs or small groups to accomplish shared goals. They build together, discuss together, and present together. They teach each other and learn from one another. Success as a group is celebrated. Positive interdependence promotes individual and group learning.

Interactive learning not only helps people learn but also helps learners feel better about themselves and get along better with others. It accomplishes these things more effectively than the independent or competitive methods.

Here's a selection of interactive learning techniques that are used in Group's Core Belief Bible Study Series. With any of these models, leaders may assign students to specific partners or small groups. This will maximize cooperation and learning by preventing all the "rowdies" from linking up. And it will allow for new friendships to form outside of established cliques.

Following any period of partner or small-group work, the leader may reconvene the entire class for large-group processing. During this time the teacher may ask for reports or discoveries from individuals or teams. This technique builds in accountability for the teacherless pairs and small groups.

Pair-Share—With this technique each student turns to a partner and responds to a question or problem from the teacher or leader. Every learner responds. There are no passive observers. The teacher may then ask people to share their partners' responses.

Study Partners—Most curricula and most teachers call for Scripture passages to be read to the whole class by one person. One reads; the others doze.

Why not relinquish some teacher control and let partners read and react with each other? They'll all be involved—and will learn more.

Learning Groups—Students work together in small groups to create a model, design artwork, or study a passage or story; then they discuss what they learned through the experience. Each person in the learning group may be assigned a specific role. Here are some examples:

Reader

Recorder (makes notes of key thoughts expressed during the reading or discussion)

Checker (makes sure everyone understands and agrees with answers arrived at by the group)

Encourager (urges silent members to share their thoughts)

When everyone has a specific responsibility, knows what it is, and contributes to a small group, much is accomplished and much is learned.

Summary Partners—One student reads a paragraph, then the partner summarizes the paragraph or interprets its meaning. Partners alternate roles with each paragraph.

The paraphrasing technique also works well in discussions. Anyone who wishes to share a thought must first paraphrase what the previous person said. This sharpens listening skills and demonstrates the power of feedback communication.

Jigsaw—Each person in a small group examines a different concept, Scripture, or part of an issue. Then each teaches the others in the group. Thus, all members teach, and all must learn the others' discoveries. This technique is called a jigsaw because individuals are responsible to their group for different pieces of the puzzle.

JIGSAW EXAMPLE

Here's an example of a jigsaw.

Assign four-person teams. Have teammates each number off from one to four. Have all the Ones go to one corner of the room, all the Twos to another corner, and so on.

Tell team members they're responsible for learning information in their numbered corners and then for teaching their team members when they return to their original teams.

Give the following assignments to various groups:

Ones: Read Psalm 22. Discuss and list the prophecies made about Jesus.

Twos: Read Isaiah 52:13–53:12. Discuss and list the prophecies made about Jesus.

Threes: Read Matthew 27:1-32. Discuss and list the things that happened to Jesus.

Fours: Read Matthew 27:33-66. Discuss and list the things that happened to Jesus.

After the corner groups meet and discuss, instruct all learners to return to their original teams and report what they've learned. Then have each team determine which prophecies about Jesus were fulfilled in the passages from Matthew.

Call on various individuals in each team to report one or two prophecies that were fulfilled.

You Can Do It Too!

All this information may sound revolutionary to you, but it's really not. God has been using active and interactive learning to teach his people for generations. Just look at Abraham and Isaac, Jacob and Esau, Moses and the Israelites, Ruth and Boaz. And then there's Jesus, who used active learning all the time!

Group's Core Belief Bible Study Series makes it easy for you to use active and interactive learning with your group. The active and interactive elements are automatically built in! Just follow the outlines, and watch as your kids grow through experience and positive interaction with others.

FOR DEEPER STUDY

For more information on incorporating active and interactive learning into your work with teenagers, check out these resources:

● *Why Nobody Learns Much of Anything at Church: And How to Fix It,* by Thom and Joani Schultz (Group Publishing) and
● *Do It! Active Learning in Youth Ministry,* by Thom and Joani Schultz (Group Publishing).

your evaluation of

Bible Study Series
for junior high/middle school

the truth about
GOD

Group Publishing, Inc.
Attention: Core Belief Talk-back
P.O. Box 481
Loveland, CO 80539
Fax: (970) 669-1994

Please help us continue to provide innovative and useful resources for ministry. After you've led the studies in this volume, take a moment to fill out this evaluation; then mail or fax it to us at the address above. Thanks!

● ● ● ● ● ●

1. As a whole, this book has been (circle one)

not very helpful   very helpful
1   2   3   4   5   6   7   8   9   10

2. The best things about this book:

3. How this book could be improved:

4. What I will change because of this book:

5. Would you be interested in field-testing future Core Belief Bible Studies and giving us your feedback? If so, please complete the information below:

Name _____

Street address _____

City _____ State _____ Zip _____

Daytime telephone (____) _____ Date _____

THANKS!